I Care for My Friend

My Friend

Katie Peters

GRL Consultants,
Diane Craig and Monica Marx,
Certified Literacy Specialists

Lerner Publications ◆ Minneapolis

Note from a GRL Consultant
This Pull Ahead leveled book has been carefully designed for beginning readers.
A team of guided reading literacy experts has reviewed and leveled the book to
ensure readers pull ahead and experience success.

Lerner Publications
An imprint of Lerner Publishing Group, Inc.
241 First Avenue North
Minneapolis, MN 55401 USA

For reading levels and more information, look up this title at www.lernerbooks.com.

Main body text set in Memphis Pro 24/39
Typeface provided by Linotype.

Photo Acknowledgments
The images in this book are used with the permission of: © A3pfamily/Shutterstock Images,
pp. 8–9; © Evgeny Karandaev/Shutterstock Images, p. 3; © InesBazdar/Shutterstock
Images, pp. 10–11, 16 (right); © MNStudio/Shutterstock Images, pp. 14–15; © Monkey
Business Images/Shutterstock Images, pp. 12–13; © Robert Kneschke/Shutterstock Images,
pp. 4–5, 16 (left); © Spotmatik Ltd/Shutterstock Images, pp. 6–7, 16 (center).

Front cover: © mae_chaba/Shutterstock Images.

Library of Congress Cataloging-in-Publication Data

Names: Peters, Katie, author.
Title: I care for my friend / Katie Peters.
Description: Minneapolis, MN : Lerner Publications , [2023] | Series: I care (Pull Ahead
    Readers People Smarts—nonfiction) | Includes index. | Audience: Ages 4–7 | Audience:
    Grades K–1 | Summary: "Friends like to play, share, and laugh with one another. Early
    readers can explore ways to care for a friend in this easily accessible text. Pairs with the
    fiction book, Kaleo Helps"— Provided by publisher.
Identifiers: LCCN 2021044339 (print) | LCCN 2021044340 (ebook) | ISBN 9781728457628
    (library binding) | ISBN 9781728461519 (ebook)
Subjects: LCSH: Friendship in children—Juvenile literature. | Friendship—Juvenile
    literature. | Caring—Juvenile literature.
Classification: LCC HQ784.F7 .P48 2023 (print) | LCC HQ784.F7 (ebook) | DDC 302.34083—dc23

LC record available at https://lccn.loc.gov/2021044339
LC ebook record available at https://lccn.loc.gov/2021044340

Manufactured in the United States of America
1 – CG – 7/15/22

Contents

I Care for My Friend

I play with my friend.

I ride with my friend.

I share with my friend.

I talk with my friend.

I laugh with my friend.

I care for my friend.

Can you think of a time when you helped a friend?

Did You See It?

ball

bike

book

Index